Empowerment

Gaining Knowledge for Financial Improvement

by Mary Brouillette

Published by Earthgirl Ventures
c/o Amazon Publishing

First Printing: 12/2019

TO REACH THE AUTHOR AND ORDER MORE COPIES:

EARTHGIRL VENTURES

www.ProjectRentNoMore.com

Earthgirlventures@gmail.com

Printed in the United States of America

ISBN: 9781700132635

Empowerment

Gaining Knowledge for Financial Improvement

Acknowledgements

"I would like to thank everyone that contributed knowledge in teaching classes and helping me with content for this book. You all show a great desire to help others, educate them, and give hope, as well as proof, that it does not matter where you come from or what you do that defines who you are. It is what you make of yourself and your life.

Knowledge is power. I truly believe that with knowledge, we continue to grow and advance in our lives."

Mary teaches free classes several times a month from homebuyer education to credit and building wealth. She is co-host of a syndicated radio talk show on Sunday Mornings called Money Talk, branch manager of a local mortgage company, public speaker, trainer, and entrepreneur, and featured in various training videos on YouTube and various other social media outlets.

Her desire is to reach as many people and help them as possible and to give them a few tools for self-improvement and empowerment along the way.

Specialty information provided by Terrence Hawkins and Matthew Carpenter.

Dedication

To all the seekers of continual knowledge and to my family, close friends, and my rockstar coach, Tim Davis:

Thank you. Without your encouragement and patience, I would have never completed my book.

FEAR AND
LACK
OF
KNOWLEDGE
WILL KEEP
YOU
STAGNANT
RIGHT WHERE
YOU ARE

Complacency: *Careless Contentment with Where You Are Right Now*

A feeling of smug or uncritical satisfaction with one's achievements...or lack thereof...

We often say or think we cannot go any farther in life than where we are and that where we come from should matter.

I say, STOP! You control your life and your destiny by what you believe. Stop believing you are not enough. If you are of faith and of Christ, stand up and believe you are ENOUGH as Christ runs through you and works through you. He believed enough in YOU to die on the cross. Open your thoughts and your mind and take control. Reteach yourself and believe you can achieve more...that you are MORE!

If you remain in the same spot, you will always be in the same place in life. Make more of yourself as you do not know what you can achieve until you get up and try.

How far can a rubber band stretch before it snaps?

Stretch one out and see. You never know, do you?

It is by far easier to stay in the same rut day to day where we know what will happen than it is to step out of the comfort zone and try something new.

It is the fear of not knowing what will happen or if we will succeed or fail. It is OK to FALL! Learn from the mistake and grow. Try again and keep trying until you make it!

Those who choose complacency never advance. They never change their habits and never move from where they are to where they dream of being.

Take my challenge.

Step out into the world.

Make changes everyday to get you on the path to what you want out of life.

Live everyday to the fullest.

...and when you finally succeed, never forget your journey!

Preface

In this day and time, it never ceases to amaze me what as a general public, we just do not know and are not taught in school. This has sprouted many relationships for me in an endeavor to educate on financial matters and help people learn how credit and finances work, what makes them tick, and how to position ourselves and our generations to come for a better tomorrow.

I have always been taught to have my hands in more than one cookie jar but until I was much older and the market crashed, did not realize how important that lesson really was.

I have always loved helping people learn and grow and over the past several years, I have taught many workshops from homebuyer education to credit and finances, programs to help people, to changing one's mindset to change their future outcome.

This book is a compilation of the information I have been teaching on my own, as well as with other professionals, in the hopes of enriching, just one person's lifestyle.

CHANGE YOUR MINDSET, CHANGE YOUR LIFE -
Gerald G. Jampolsky

DARE TO DREAM

DARE TO BELIEVE

STRIVE TO ACHIEVE

...AND IF YOU FALL

GET UP!

TABLE OF CONTENTS

Introduction

It is my sincere hope to be able to share my knowledge and teach you something you did not already know and to leave you with a few tools to assist along the way.

I then hope you find it within yourself to share the knowledge you learn to empower someone else to inspire them to change or enhance their lives as well.

We will cover everything financial in a beginner to intermediate stage to help kickstart your life and get you to the next level.

Chapter 1:

What You Have Not Been Taught About Credit

CREDIT

Credit is the basis of everything we do in life. Even though it should not define us, for many, it does. Credit is our ability to have, manage, and repay debt and there are 2 types of credit- open ended and close ended.

Let's begin with open ended. Open ended credit is like a revolving door. You are assigned a limit that you do not have to completely use up and if you pay it completely off, it is still there to use again and again. This type of credit comes in the form of credit cards and makes up 30% of our score. Therefore, if you do not have a credit card, you are missing 30% of your equation. This form of credit also gives life and longevity to your score as you can keep it open your entire lifetime as long as you take care of it and manage it correctly.

For example, in my classes, I ask people if I give someone a card with a $1000 limit and they do no use it and give someone else that same card but they use $500, which one gets the most points when the card company updates your credit report. Most people will point to the person that uses the $500, but in reality, it is a catch 22. They both get "0." If you do not use the credit, I have nothing to update and it costs roughly $6-$8 per bureau to update the bureaus so if I am not collecting money from them, I am not going to pay to update the report. On the other hand, if they spent $500, they are at a 50% utilization and it could go either way. Most of the time it continues to increase so I update the credit but do not award any points.

Most folks will advise a 30% utilization but if you are opening new credit, particularly unsecured credit, a 10% usage is enough that the creditor has to report to the bureaus and you are using the credit and managing it, so you get points awarded. Keep in mind, though, that it can take up to 6 months to see that though as the company wants to see your track record.

When folks do not have this piece of the puzzle, I recommend a secured credit card that will report to all 3 bureaus. With a secured card, you give a deposit that becomes your credit limit so no risk to the creditor and they start you with points. The trick is to get at least a $300 credit limit but to only use $30-$35 per month maximum. The first month you get the card and activate it, they will usually charge an annual fee of between $24-$35. Activate the card but do not use it that month. Wait for the bill and pay. Then go get a tank of gas or something small and put the card away. You would do this anyway so also put the money away for this until the bill comes in and pay it. In this practice, you teach yourself good skills for maintaining your account and you will get a lot of points to help your credit whether you are just starting out or rebuilding your credit. Also, after a year of good history, most companies will send your deposit back to you and make it an unsecured card.

The next type of credit is closed ended. These are installment loans like car payments, student loans, personal loans, or even mortgages. The loans are what they are. You spend "X" amount of money and the loan is "X" amount. You create history and get points for paying on time or ahead but once you pay them in full, they are done and closed. You lose all that history as the accounts have nothing left to update.

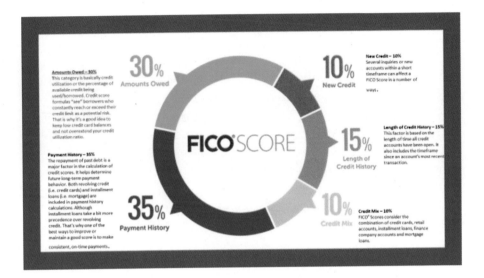

Credit is made up of 5 components:

- Payment History

- Credit Utilization

- Length of Credit History

- New Credit

- Credit Mix

Payment history is self-explanatory. You either pay on time or you do not. You pay the minimum payment, or you pay extra.

Credit Utilization is where credit cards come into play. Do you pay the minimum or more? Do you pay to zero? Are you over 50% of your credit limit? Are you over the limit? Do you pay on time or late? This category actually makes up 30% of your credit score.

Length of Credit History reflects how long you have had reporting tradelines and is also another space that credit cards come into play. Cars, loans, and even mortgages eventually get paid in full and will stop updating. Credit cards can remain open and reporting for a lifetime if you handle them properly.

New credit weighs a bit in too. You never need 30 tradelines. I see people open cards and get intermediate loans like candy. Every time you apply for credit, you get an inquiry and lose points. Every new account needs to see how you manage it and build the history. Be sure to keep down applications for new credit as much as you can.

Credit Mix is having balance. You need at least 1 closed ended credit line and 1-2 open ended lines or credit cards. Credit cards like Mastercard and Visa that can be used anywhere will also carry a little more weight than ones for department stores that can only be used in 1 particular store.

Great credit begins with understanding what credit is made of and achieving habits to use credit wisely.

You must learn that when life happens, if you just communicate with the creditors, they will try to find ways to help you not go into default or collection. Also, occasionally, mistakes in reporting are made.

Also, student loans are the easiest entities to work with and should never be in default. When you are in trouble, communication is key.

This is for any type of credit, but the student loan servicers are there to help you and have many options to help you stay out of default. They have income-based repayments that can be as low as $0 per month, forbearance where no payments are due and can be renewed in 12-month increments, as well as extended payments to help lower what you pay monthly. If you do mess up and end up in default, call them. These loans do not magically disappear and will follow you everywhere you go. Most servicers will help you set up a repayment plan with payments as low as $5 per month and after 6-9 payments on time, the loan comes out of default status. At this time, if you are still struggling, you can apply for reduced or income-based payments or even forbearance.

Under the Fair Credit Reporting Act (FRCA), these can be corrected, and you have the right to request debts be validated and if they cannot be validated, they must be removed from your credit. Under this law creditors must respond within 30 days of your request in writing.

However, credit repair is a gamble. There is no magic crystal ball that can guarantee results. However, the law allows credit validation. What is the difference, you ask?

Credit validation is where a creditor is asked to provide specific documentation pieces to verify they legally have a right to place items on your credit.

For example, if you open any type of credit or apply, there is a signature required. They have to prove you signed for the application. There are usually several articles of information they must provide, depending on type of account, to verify it belongs to you and can be placed on your credit report.

If they do not have the correct pieces of information, the account must be removed.

However, if you are using a free credit report system to track your activity and score, keep in mind that a lot of times you are waving your right to the Fair Credit Reporting Act and creditors now have up to 55 days versus 30 days to respond.

It is very easy to procrastinate and not work on things as life happens. If you find yourself in this situation, there is still hope. There are a few very good, reputable companies that can help with credit challenges. Companies that assist in credit validation and restoration cannot charge upfront. They must charge in arrears and only for work that has been done. They are not allowed to charge upfront.

I have researched several over the years and found 2 companies that are good.

One is 360 Credit Consultants. A huge shout out to Matt Carpenter and his team. They have done a tremendous job working with their clients and communicating with them. They are also very reasonable.

They charge $89 to startup and then $69/month. There is no contract or cancellation fee. Use them for as long as you need them and be sure to tell others about your experience with them. You get a free consultation with them and they assign a personal counselor to hold your hand and get you through the process. They also do all the heavy lifting for you. They write the letters with all the correct verbiage to help maximize results.

Included with their service is also tips and tricks to managing your credit once back on track and ways to rebuild your credit, even after bankruptcy. Their website is full of educational information to help you win your credit journey.

The other company is MWR Financial. This one is very cool. It is a membership based financial services company. They charge $79/month with no startup fee or cancellation fee. Within their membership, you not only get credit assistance, you get debt elimination, tax filing evaluation with certified public accountants where they help you maximize how your returns are filed and access to an Enrolled Agent or "EA" that can help negotiate tax debt on your behalf, and a team of financial planners that can teach you how to build wealth for retirement using vehicles like Private Reserve Accounts where you can essentially become your own bank and Land Trusts. This is a very well-rounded company as they cover you all the way around financially.

For their credit service, you enroll and upload a copy of your credit report and identification, and they write the letters for you.

Both companies offer an add-on access to Trans Union's Smart Credit App that gives you a more accurate look at your 3 scores and monitors your accounts for activity. You can even add in your bank accounts and it monitors them for usage. If any suspicious activity is detected, you get a text and email notification within 30 seconds. This helps cut down on identity theft and fraud. They also offer correction protection in case anything gets hacked. It is like Lifelock on steroids. The add-on cost for this is roughly $20 per month and a small price to pay for peace of mind.

The Smart Credit App has literally been a lifesaver for my husband and me. He travels a lot for work and running through airports, his cards were scanned by a hacker and our banks accounts that were linked were compromised. Within 30 seconds of a transaction over $50, I receive both an email and a text to let me know where and how much incase we are hacked. I also have this on my credit cards. When someone uses a card without our permission, we are immediately shutdown until we can get to the banks and close accounts or track them down.

I will provide contact information for both companies in the Resources Section at the back of this book.

Chapter 2:

Secrets to Tax Strategies You Need to Know

So, as many of you know, individuals with home offices and W2 income lost their write-off's this past year. No more *Unreimbursed Job Expenses.*

This is where a Home-Based Business is very helpful. There are over 180 possible deductions available for a legitimate home business. You just have to have the intent that you are doing the business to make a profit and that the business is worked from a dedicated space in your home.

Here are a few of the items you may not know that you can deduct: Children between the ages of 7 to 17. You can employ them to work for your business and pay them as your employees. You can pay them up to the standard deduction annually which is $12,200 in 2019. (It will go up even higher in 2020). It is a tax deduction for you as an employee and tax-free money to them. It is a great way to teach them to earn and manage money, build character, and learn responsibility.

I had my daughter clean my office, file my documents, and as she matured, help with my marketing and social media. With the money she earned, she paid her cell phone bill and bought school supplies. It was a win-win. She earned her own money and bought her own things, so they were no longer disposable. She took care of her belongings. As for me, I had an employee that helped me with things I did not necessarily enjoy doing and cut my personal expenses a bit as she paid her own way.

Mileage is another huge one. This one is actually a tax credit that reduces your taxable income from the home-based business. Miles driven to work your business can be used in this credit. Your commuting miles to your regular job can possibly be deducted. Mileage to even Walmart can be deducted if you are intending to pick up office supplies and you can even maximize time and buy your groceries while you are there.

Here is the power of just mileage when you "own" a business. Most Americans drive a minimum of 26,000 miles per year. IRS up through 2018 gave .54 per mile and in 2019, it goes up to .58 per mile. On a low side, let's say you fall into an 18% tax bracket. Look at the math:

26,000 miles x .54= $14,040 x 18% tax bracket= $2572.20/ 12 months= $210.60 per month (This is a tax credit against your taxable income which reduces how much you get taxed on, hence, extra money.)

Other deductions include cellphone bills, health insurance premiums, travel expenses for business trips, and cost of business meals. You can also deduct a portion of your utilities and rent/mortgage as the expense of a home office.

There are also several apps you can download to help track all these things for you. Taxbot is one such application. It tracks your mileage automatically and you just have to open it and swipe left or right to tell it business or personal miles. Taxbot can also keep track of expenses by you simply snapping pictures of your receipts and you can enter income as you receive it. It helps keep all your records handy for tax time.

There are so many possibilities and you should always consult a tax professional.

Here is a page that can give you an idea of what having a business can do for you: www.myinstantpayraise.com. This page was originally written by Terrence Hawkins of Hawkins Accounting and Tax Service located in Charlotte, NC. Terrence and his wife, Pam, are 2 of the most knowable tax professionals I have ever met and specialize in home-based and small businesses. (Also, you do not have to live in Charlotte to use their services.) Terrence is an Enrolled Agent licensed in all 50 states to negotiate tax debt with the IRS. I have highly recommended Hawkins Accounting and Tax for many years as they not only do taxes, they educate.

They also make you feel like family as soon as you start working with them and always try to find the most benefits to help you in all your tax and accounting needs.

Terrence has been working on taxes since we were teenagers. His dad had an accounting firm and later Terrence and his wife opened theirs. They definitely have heart and passion for what they do and are well known throughout the country for their work and all the education they provide.

Terrence has given many speeches and still does several conventions every year. He is also a host on ESPN Charlotte's Radio Show Coffee and Cash Flow.

Chapter 3:

Don't Let Money Stop You From Achieving Your Future

Finally, we will talk about money. This is what makes the world tick.

There are so many things to learn: how to save, how to invest, how to grow it, how to make ends meet when you are down and out. Hopefully, by the time you finish this section, you will have gained some knowledge on these subjects and ideas to implement to make a better future.

Debt is just that...Debt. You either build wealth or you build debt. A large portion of the population builds debt.

We must learn to take control of our finances and eliminate debt. As we discussed earlier, debt and lack of funds, contributes to our financial and credit crisis. It is easier for us to spend than to save.

The rule of thumb I have always taught my students is it is better to shop if you can pay cash for the items you purchase. If you implement that into your shopping habits, you will find you focus more on what you need versus what you merely want. This, you stay out of debt woes.

If you eat out a lot, try planning meals for the week at home and precooking them or cut out one restaurant or fast food meal a week and put the money you would have spent into a savings account or investment account.

So, let's build upon this a bit. I have always preached to pay yourself first. You are important too. Ration out a percentage of your earnings each pay period that is for you specifically. This is what you have for gas, eating out, and incidentals. Start a coffee fund where you even put a little of that money away for emergencies or vacations. In the old days, we would put this in a coffee can. In today's times, I say visit a credit union and start an account just for this or even look at apps like Stash or Acorns to help. They even start you with a small amount of free money to open an account.

While both Stash and Acorns are very similar, Stash is my personal favorite. They give you $5 free just to sign up. You can then invest in stocks to grow your money. They allow you to purchase single stocks or a mixed portfolio of stocks without having full face value all at once or trading fees. You simply purchase the portions you can afford at a given time. They also have lots of educational materials to teach budgeting and investing tips. They also have a retirement account that works similarly to the savings plan and a debit card that you can add funds to or set up with direct deposit. With the debit card, every purchase you make earns you some stock. If you shop at Amazon and use the Stash debit card to pay, you earn Amazon stock with your purchase. It can also tag to your other banking accounts and be set to grab the rounded-up amounts. Each time you shop or spend, it will round up those accounts at the end of the day and invest the funds in stocks you choose.

Mint is another free app that is similar to Quicken or Quickbooks and is designed by Intuit. It can help manage your bank accounts, investments, teach you budgeting and saving, and keep track of your expenses.

Creating a budget will help pinpoint the amounts you have to allocate towards paying yourself and saving. Budgets do not have to be complex. Start by listing all your creditors and the amounts you pay to each monthly. Next organize them by the dates they need to be paid and align your pay dates with the bill due dates. The amount you have leftover is what you have to pay yourself, invest in the future, tithe, or add extra to your bill payments to pay down balances faster. You would be really amazed at what even $10 above a minimum payment can do to alleviate the balance you owe.

There is a parable in Matthews, Chapter 25, about a master who was leaving his home and entrusted 3 of his servants with 8 talents divided amongst them based upon their abilities. One was given 5 talents, another was given 2 talents, and the last one was left 1 talent. They were told to invest and grow their talents. In his absence and in return for what they were entrusted with would be doubled as their reward.

When the master returned from his travels, the servants were called to him to give account of what they accomplished. The first one who was given 5 talents, had traded them and made 5 more talents. The second one who was given 2 talents also gained 2 additional talents. The master commended them for their valiant efforts and they were given a positive reward. The third one, however, was afraid and took the talent he was given and buried it for safe keeping. The master chastised him and took away his talent and had him cast out for if he was not going to invest it, he could have placed it in the bank to grow interest.

Many valuable lessons can be learned from this story. It teaches us to work, invest, learn, and how to grow and save. These are the fundamental building blocks of life. Everything we teach is designed to help get, build, and manage wealth and have something to leave behind to our upcoming generations.

I know. I know, what if you do not have "extra" money and what if you do not even have income?

I found the internet to be a huge resource on this. Look at all the things you can find that give you money when you need it:

1) Apps that pay you for tasks. When you are down and out or need extra income, there are apps and companies that will pay you to do various tasks. Here are a few:

- **Lyft or Uber**- Pays you to drive people around town
- **TomAsk** (iphone users only)- Pays you to

download apps and open them within 3 minutes. Easily make up to $10 per day within a few minutes of your time
- **Foap** and **Clashot**- Pay you for pictures you take
- **Fiverr**- Freelance Job Site- Post Your Skill and How Much You Charge to Get Jobs
- **Shipt**- Get pay to deliver people's groceries
- Produce Box- Pays you to deliver fresh fruits and vegetables to people
- **DoorDash**- Pays you to deliver food
- **Scribie**- Pays you to transcribe audio online. $1 for every 6 minutes of audio transcribed
- **Rev.com**- Get paid to be a transcriptionist. Can pay up to $50/hr
- **Blogmott**- Pays you to write blogs
- Takelessons.com and Voices.com- Pays you to give singing lessons or do voice overs
- **TryMyUI** and **Analysia**- Pays you to test websites
- Arise- Pays you to do office tasks from home or to do customer service from home
- Money App- Pays you to do tasks like taking surveys, checking out store displays, giving feedback, and testing services
- **CreditCardBroker**- Affiliate marketing for credit card offers. Give out your link on social media, personal websites, or blogs an earn cash everytime someone signs up. Free to join and they will even build a landing page for you to use.
  https://partners.creditcardbroker.com/signup/4374
(Affiliate marketing in general is a great way to make easy money and create cash flow on autopilot. The

hardest part is the initial set up to get your link exposed and then it grows from there.)

The opportunities are endless!

2) Apps that pay you cashback for shopping with your favorite merchants:
    - **TopCashBack**- Shop online with the stores you love and get money back for each purchase. Retailers like Ebay, Amazon, Walmart, Target, American Eagle, Best Buy, AliExpress, and even travel sites such as Marriott Bonvoy or Expedia are listed. This site is free and they even start you with a free $10 using this link: http://www.topcashback.com/ref/Member71014 9341111
    - **MyPoints, Rakuten, and Ebates** are other sites that pay you to join free and shop with your favorite merchants.
    - **Ibotta** and **Checkout51**- Pay you to upload grocery receipts
    - **GetUpside**- Earn cashback on gas purchases. Use code CJRWP to earn an extra
    - **CoinOut**- Pays cashback on any purchase anywhere. Shop. Pay. Scan your receipt and get cash back to your Amazon, Paypal, or Bank Account.
    - Fetch Rewards- Works just like CoinOut. Shop as normal and upload receipts to earn cash back.

3) **Truebill & Budget Tracker** and **Trim**- Tracks your expenses and negotiates lower bills when possible and can cancel services you are paying for but forgot about or are no longer using. Really helps save you money.

4) Sell items you do not use for extra cash- Craigslist, Letgo, or OfferUp.
5) If you are crafty, sell your crafts online with sites like Etsy, Ecwid, and Shopify.

There are so many ways to make extra money and some with very little effort that it does not make sense to be broke. Start small and build up. Somethings build up as you dive in and some things build residual income that requires no effort to run once it ignites.

If you can search the internet or download an app, you can find ways to make money and grow your financial portfolio. You always need a backup and more importantly, one that you control. When someone else controls your earnings, they can shut it off at any time and without notice. Always, always, always have a Plan B. I learned this years ago from my family friend and tax accountant, Terrence Hawkins.

Think like a business owner or boss and take steps to enhance or enrich your current lifestyle. Even if you had "job" security, it never hurts to do something for yourself that can end up replacing your current income, put you in control of your future and more importantly, your time.

In 1999, I sold Real Estate and then migrated to mortgages. I was on top of the world! Then 2007 came and the market began to crash. In 2009, it fully plummeted, and I was left without income. Had it not been for my many other talents, I would have starved.

My daughter was in high school at the time and we were nearly broke. I lost my house and moved in with my sister. I took odd jobs working on other people's cars and cleaning people's houses just to stay afloat. Then I found a job working at a gold buying kiosk that got us on track and worked my way up to becoming the district manager. It really pulled me back up on my feet until the market recovered.

Had I not had other ways to earn money, we would have been in a lot more trouble.

Since then, I have joined a few companies that are MLM based but ones that are sustainable and offer products or services that I need and use and that others also need and can benefit from. MLM, if the right type of business, can result in great amounts of passive or residual income. This is money made without extra work once the initial groundwork is laid.

One of the companies, doTerra, provides me with essential oils to stay healthy and out of the doctor's office so much and grew just from me sharing how the oils and supplements have helped me. This one actually has grown enough to almost cover my "habit" or pay for my daily supplements, although, I do end up giving away more than I sell as it is all about helping others any way possible. I have a very good friend that always says, "Health is your Wealth!"

Another company is one I previously mentioned, MWR Financial. This one has actually grown to where I not only help others, but I am making enough to pay for all my traditional marketing for my mortgage business. This company offers a membership that helps with credit errors, getting out of debt faster, finding tax benefits most people do not know exist and ensuring that taxes are filed correctly, and building wealth for the future that can be left to your younger generations. It aligns with professionals in each area of financial well-being that share their knowledge and teach others how to accomplish their financial goals along with an opportunity to share the services and benefits with others while either getting their membership free or earning extra money as business advocate.

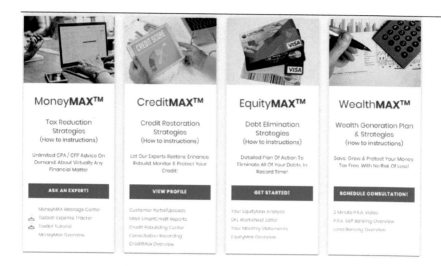

MoneyMAX™	CreditMAX™	EquityMAX™	WealthMAX™
Tax Reduction Strategies (How to instructions)	Credit Restoration Strategies (How to instructions)	Debt Elimination Strategies (How to instructions)	Wealth Generation Plan & Strategies (How to instructions)
Unlimited CPA / CFP Advice On Demand, About Virtually Any Financial Matter	Let Our Experts Restore, Enhance, Rebuild, Monitor & Protect Your Credit!	Detailed Plan Of Action To Eliminate All Of Your Debts, In Record Time!	Save, Grow & Protect Your Money, Tax Free, With No Risk Of Loss!
ASK AN EXPERT!	**VIEW PROFILE**	**GET STARTED!**	**SCHEDULE CONSULTATION!**
MoneyMAX Message Center	Customer Portal/Uploads	Your EquityMax Analysis	2 Minute P.R.A. Video
Taxbot- Expense Tracker	MWR SmartCredit Reports	DHL Worksheet Editor	P.R.A. Self Banking Overview
TaxBot Tutorial	Credit Rebuilding Center	Your Monthly Statements	Land Banking Overview
MoneyMax Overview	Consultation Recording	EquityMax Overview	
	CreditMax Overview		

If Terrence had not taught me all the money matters that he has over the years, I do not know where I would be today. I am thankful to have him in my life and for him to share his wisdom.

Now I teach classes locally to educate others and am part of a radio show where I can give out weekly tips and tidbits. I compiled this book to help spread the word on a larger scale as we just do not know what we do not know.

Ecclesiastes 7:12- For the protection of money, and the advantage of knowledge is that wisdom preserves the life of him who has it.

Bonus: Tidbit on Affiliate Marketing, which like MLM, can end up producing income passively and on autopilot:

If you look at the bottom of most business websites, like Amazon, even credit card sites, or Walmart, there are links to either partner with them or to sign up as an Affiliate Marketer. For some of them, you do not even need a website of your own. You just need to find places to place small free ads and when people click the ad to learn more and make a purchase or sign up, you get paid a commission or fee for driving the business to that entity. It is easier than you think to get started.

With Amazon, you sign up to as an affiliate and choose items to promote using a Blog site or social media platform like Pinterest, Facebook, or Instagram. If someone clicks through your link and purchases, you earn 10% of the sale. However, if they use your link and do not buy that item but still make a purchase on Amazon, you still earn a commission. Pretty cool, right?

Clickbank is another platform. They sell ebooks and software on various businesses and topics. When you promote products on their site and someone purchases from your links, you get paid.

These types of income paths will not make you rich overnight but can add up to some amazing extra cash over time.

There are also sites that will give you totally free full size product samples to try out if you promise to leave a review on the items you test out. PinchMe is a favorite of mine. They send out on Tuesdays ad the samples are on a first come, first serve basis

Another way to save versus the traditional way is through Cash Value Life Insurance (CVLI). This is not your traditional life policy like mom and dad have from back in the day. However, it has been around since 1880. No one ever thinks of it as an option because they do not understand it.

My friend, Steven Crawford with FIG Wealth and Retirement, was the one who introduced me to this concept. The policy I have gives a guarantee of a 5% return on every deposit I make and it accrues value over time. There is no cap to what I can contribute, no matter how much money I earn annually. This is also guaranteed for 5 years.

It was a no brainer for me. I even rolled my IRA over to it. Here's the thing, if I needed money for an emergency, I could withdraw funds at any time. However, in my IRA or even a 401K, someone else tells me how much I can or cannot access and then there is a tax penalty of up to 10% if I withdraw before the age of 59 ½. There are also a lot of other stipulations on IRA's and 401k's, but if it is my money and I am in a pinch and need it, I want to access it...all of it that is needed.

Did you know that Ray Croc that founded what we know today as McDonald's financed his startup using funds from his CVLI policy?

Crazy, isn't it? You should call my friend and ask him. He consults folks all over the country too.

Steven has been featured in Forbes Magazine and co-authored a book called The Success Formula with Jack Canfield of Chicken Soup. He is also a host on the ESPN Charlotte Radio Show Coffee and Cashflow.

Don't worry. I will give you his contact information in the back of the book shortly.

Chapter 4:

Resources

www.hawkinstax.net

704-509-2399

Matt Carpenter

512-539-6130

matt@360creditconsulting.com

www.360creditconsulting.com

www.makewealthreal.com/bedebtfree

www.mwrfinancial.com/bedebtfree

Membership includes access to several financial services to help you secure your future. Services include improving credit, maximizing tax benefits and review of previous tax returns, debt elimination, and strategies/outlets to build wealth through a team of industry professionals.

www.figwealthadvisors.com
980-216-8487

https://get.stashinvest.com/mary8j4uv

Secured Card Links to Rebuild Credit

https://www.creditbuildercard.com/egp.html

https://www.creditcardbroker.com/promos/feed4374
(fyi, First Latitude does not charge an annual fee)

Remember, the key to the secured cards is to do at least a $300 limit and then only use $30-$35 per month and pay in full when you receive the bill. The first bill will usually include an annual fee so I recommend just activating it and waiting for the bill to come in.

About the Author

Mary Brouillette was born in the outskirts of Charlotte, NC. Her family struggled to make ends meet but taught her to always work hard and strive for more.

During her high school years, she worked at McDonald's and went from a cashier to shift manager to the store trading area representative. She learned to manage people of different age groups, how to start and maintain public relations, and basic marketing skills. Little did she know that skills would resonate within her throughout life.

She was always shy but caring, always looking out for others before herself. At the age of 26, a widow and single mother, she began her own homebuying adventure and met many souls who desired to help others more than themselves. Through their collective efforts, she was able to purchase her first home.

The selling agent was attempting to open his own real estate company at that time and asked her if she ever thought about becoming an agent. He then helped her find a school to begin her journey.

After a few years, she became a Broker-In-Charge of one of his offices and then the company bought a mortgage company. The real estate firm had all the Brokers-In-Charge obtain mortgage licenses and she quickly learned everything started there.

Mary then began to switch gears and go the mortgage consultant way and was known as the loan officer that never said "No." She would either find a solution or give clients a game plan.

To this very day, she continues to do just that. *"It has never been about the money but rather helping people. Someone had to do this for me, and it is my way to give back."*

Connect with the Author

Mchaney12@gmail.com

https://www.facebook.com/mary.chaney2

https://fb.me/ProjectRentNoMoreCharlotteTeam

https://www.linkedin.com/in/marychaney/

https://www.instagram.com/mchaney52/

https://www.youtube.com/channel/UCB9quOD6YJtDCjqIJuoro3A

https://www.pinterest.com/marychaney2/pins/

https://projectrentnomore.tumblr.com/

Listen to our Podcasts:

https://soundcloud.com/mary-chaney-brouillette

https://www.tumblr.com/blog/projectrentnomore

Coming soon....

www.projectrentnomore.com

STAY TUNED FOR THE NEXT PART OF THIS SERIES!

Made in the USA
Columbia, SC
03 January 2020